Stop Overthinking

How to Stop Worrying, Relieve Anxiety and Emotional Stress, Stop Negative Thinking.

Allison Collins

Table of the Contents:

Introduction 7

What Is Emotional Intelligence? 13

Primary and Secondary Emotions 16

Managing Negative Emotions 22

Negative Emotions 23

Negative Emotions Aren't Actually Negative 25

Turning the Negative into Positive 29

Self-Compassion 32

Emotional Intelligence 32

Positive Factors 35

Biological Relationships 35

Bouncing Back 36

Setbacks Make Us Stronger 37

Anxiety 39

Causes Of Anxiety 41

Anger as a trigger for Anxiety 47

How to Overcome Stress 51

Self-confidence and Fear 51

Self-confidence and Stress 52

How to Overcome Stress 53

Slow down time 53

You are not a superhero 54

Acknowledge that your memory is not accurate......54

Positive self-talk..55

Positive mindset...55

Get rid of self-doubt...56

Become curious 57

Embrace the fear 57

Treat all situations as if they are your choice............58

Be resourceful 58

Be grateful for criticism......................................58

Use the fear of failure to succeed 59

Take control of your thoughts 59

There is always calm at the center of a storm...........60

Get rid of your mediocre behaviors 60

Act while in the state of fear................................61

Don't avoid problems; seek them..........................61

In self-confidence, the majority never win...............62

What doesn't increase you takes from you 63

Relax 64

Set goals 64

Help out 64

Take a different viewpoint.....................................65

Try new ideas 65

Overcoming Negative Feelings..............................66

Negative Emotions Instances 69

Negative Emotions And Why We Have Them 73

CBT Strategies 74

Strategies to Eliminate Stress 78

Regular Mindfulness Exercise 97

Increased Mental Health 98

Increased Physical Health 99

Increase Overall Well-Being 99

Deep Breathing 102

Body Scan 104

Create a Safe Place 107

The Compassionate State 109

Flowing Compassion 111

Focusing Compassion Inward 113

The important habits that can change your life 117

Conclusion 128

Introduction

Today everyone is in a race for success. But no one actually takes the right steps towards achieving it. We have to make up our minds to understand the core points of success. Emotional intelligence or emotional agility? Both have the same literal meaning but have a huge role in the process of our success.

Emotional intelligence is our ability to understand emotions in ourselves and others, understand their consequences, and use that knowledge to direct our thoughts and behaviors. Since emotionally intelligent people tend to get along with others better and be more empathetic and caring, they are likely to be more effective than their counterparts. And that makes it worth learning more about emotional intelligence.

Emotional Intelligence has grown to be a popular phrase over the past decade. Everyone is talking about how important it is when it comes to enjoying professional success and fulfilling interpersonal relationships. Yet, surprisingly, not many people seem to know what emotional intelligence, also known as emotional quotient, actually is or how to improve it.

Countless studies have made shocking revelations about how emotional quotient (EQ) is far more important than intelligence quotient (IQ) when it comes to not just success at work, but also in social and personal relationships. The good news is, unlike intelligence quotient (which is largely determined by genetics), emotional quotient can be constantly enhanced.

Yes, we can continue to increase our emotional intelligence through consistent exercise. Research undertaken in multiple universities across North America and Europe have indicated that while intelligence quotient accounts for only 20 percent of our success and accomplishments, emotional intelligence plays a staggering 80 percent role in it.

This simply means that if you are not able to deal with, identify and manage your emotions and the emotions of other people, you are less likely to succeed in many aspects of life. All technical skills, experience, qualification and even intelligence are important, however, people who have the ability to deal with their own emotions and other people's emotions are the type of people who quickly rise to leadership roles.

Suddenly, emotional intelligence was the buzzword that got everyone's attention, including large corporations around the world. It became one of the most crucial parameters for employees or workforce selection for hiring managers.

In a startling study, top leaders of 200 of the nation's biggest companies were carefully studied.

It emerged that they did have some characteristics in common. Corporate leaders were exceptionally good at academic knowledge, technical skills, and the ability to manage their own emotions. Surprisingly, emotional intelligence contributed twice as much to their success than all the other three factors put together. This clearly shows that intelligence alone doesn't take us too far in life unless it is backed by the ability to understand and manage our own (and other people's) emotions.

While intelligence and technical ability can ascertain if you will be a good fit for a particular industry or role, it is your ability to manage emotions that will determine how good you are at performing the role.

Another study conducted on students by Yale University Center for emotional intelligence concluded that adolescents who possess high emotional intelligence are less anxious, are seldom bogged down by depression and are less likely to resort to addictions (alcohol, drugs, cigarettes, etc.). They are also less aggressive and less likely to display signs of becoming a bully.

Their attention span is higher; they tend to be less hyper and are known to display leadership skills. These students also excel at academics and the ability to cope with challenges related to it. It is remarkable how much of an impact emotional intelligence can have on social skills, academic performance and gaining knowledge.

Does this mean that we should focu s only on emotional intelligence and not on cognitive or rational intelligence? No, not at all because both are important. However, intellectual prowess without the ability to manage emotions won't lead us on a path to success because at the end of the day we have to deal with people all the time.

Similarly, emotional intelligence without technical skills and IQ will not lead us in the right direction. If anything, emotional quotient and intelligence quotient both complement each other to ensure overall success in different spheres of an individual's life.

Contrary to what people mistakenly believe, emotional quotient is not the rival of intelligence quotient. It is an ally. Our life is a huge social construct with complex and intricately woven social dynamics. How far do you think your cognitive ability can take you?

Emotional quotient spans several areas of our mental well-being, social relationships, interpersonal equations with people and much more. People who are emotionally intelligent demonstrate better mental health and wellbeing; they are also better equipped to lead and inspire people and enjoy more rewarding personal relationships. Therefore, the ability to manage relationships more efficiently and resolve conflicts can lead to overall greater success in life.

The benefits of possessing a high emotional quotient aren't limited to our personal life alone. EQ is applicable to our professional life as well. It is often noticed that people with average intelligence often surpass those with very high intelligence to achieve unimaginable professional success. We often wonder how X has been quickly promoted into a leadership role over Y when Y is more technically knowledgeable and intelligent. The answer most probably lies in X's ability to deal with his or her and others' emotions.

According to a study conducted by the Center for Creative Leadership, 75 percent of all careers go astray owing to emotional incompetency, the inability to deal with interpersonal issues, unsatisfactory leadership skills during crisis or conflicts, the inability to inspire people's trust and failure to adapt.

The great news is your emotional quotient is not etched in stone. It isn't something that can never be altered. It takes lots of work but increasing it is pretty attainable if you are willing to put in the necessary work. Emotional intelligence can hugely impact all aspects of your life to help you enjoy greater happiness, gain contentment and improve your well-being.

Throughout this book, we'll talk about solid, powerful strategies you can start using right away for increasing your emotional quotient and social skills. It will help give you more purpose and build more productive interpersonal relationships.

What Is Emotional Intelligence?

In simple terms, emotional intelligence is recognizing emotions and leveraging on emotional information in making healthy choices.

Emotional intelligence is the capacity to recognize our emotions and regulate them, to discern the emotions of others, and to differentiate between varying emotions, using this information to facilitate thoughts and behavior in order to achieve the desired results.

Since emotional intelligence involves recognizing emotions, it is important to have an understanding of what emotions are and what types of emotions there are.

What Are Emotions?

These are mental states or feelings that occur spontaneously and not by intention. These feelings are often accompanied by physiological reactions. These occurrences are in response to our perception of what is happening or what we see or hear per-time.

Emotions help us understand our experiences. We would never know that the death of a loved one is a sad experience if we have never felt sadness. We would never know that someone destroying our lawn is an annoying experience if we have never felt angry. Feeling emotions help us categorize our experiences and react accordingly.

Positive emotions register an experience we are having or are about to have as good and worth having. When we say we look forward to the experience, it is not the experience we look forward to per sé. It is more the emotions associated with that experience that we look forward to having.

On the other hand, negative emotions alert us of unpleasant or potentially unpleasant experiences. We know we should do certain things or not do certain things if we want to avoid such experiences. For example, when we are faced with a sudden threat, we feel fear of loss or pain. The emotion of fear triggers a fight or flight reaction. What we really are trying to avoid is the loss or pain, not the occurrence itself.

Without emotions, there would be no emotional intelligence and without emotional intelligence, we would not be able to tell precisely the kinds of experiences we want to have and the kinds we don't want to have.

According to author David G. Meyers, "Emotion is made up of three components; physiological arousal, expressive behaviors, and conscious experience."

Physiological arousal means the person feeling a particular emotion will become physiologically alert. This is a point where the sense organs are stimulated to perceive. Physiological arousal is primarily controlled by a part of the brain called the reticular activating system (RAS).

Expressive behavior refers to a behavioral reaction to the perception of what is happening, or to what is seen, heard or thought. This often involves verbal and non-verbal communication of a person's emotions.

Conscious Experience refers to the awareness of a person's environment, what he sees, hears and feels as well as his thoughts.

According to Paul Ekman, there are six basic emotions and they are anger, disgust, fear, happiness, sadness, and surprise. Robert Plutchik suggests there are eight. These eight he grouped into 4 pairs of polar opposites: joy and sadness, anger and fear, trust and distrust, and surprise and anticipation.

Primary and Secondary Emotions

Emotions are grouped into primary emotions, secondary emotions, and tertiary emotions.

Primary emotions are the initial emotions felt in response to a perception. These emotions are fear, anger, sadness, joy, love, and surprise. These are the emotions you feel without thinking. They are instinctive feelings we don't plan to have. Imagine you are walking down the road in the company of a friend and a reckless cyclist runs into your friend. The emotion you likely instinctively feel is fear. Fear that your loved one may get hurt.

Primary emotions are often called transient because they disappear quickly and are replaced. They are replaced by secondary emotions and can be secondary emotions themselves.

Secondary emotions are an offshoot of primary emotions. These emotions replace primary emotions. The emotion of fear you felt when you saw your loved one getting knocked down by the reckless cyclist may be replaced by the secondary emotion of anger. You feel angry at the cyclist for causing someone you love pain.

There are so many emotions that it is considered impossible to list all emotions that exist, but below is a generally comprehensive list of human emotions and their meaning. This list contains the basic emotions, their meanings, and their related secondary and tertiary emotions. As you go through this list, try to remember times when you felt each of these emotions. Also, try to remember times when you witnessed someone else express each of the listed emotions. You can take as much time as you need.

Fear

Fear is an unpleasant feeling triggered by a sense of danger or a threat. It is the emotion we feel when we think something bad is going to happen. The primary trigger of fear is the perception of imminent pain. This could be physical pain: fear of bodily harm or hurt; or emotional pain: fear of loss, rejection or distress; or social pain: fear of disgrace, isolation or shame. We feel the emotion of fear not only for ourselves but for others as well. Fear for others can sometimes be more unpleasant to experience than fear for oneself. This is because we usually can't control what happens to others.

Fear ranges from a little scare accompanied by mild muscular stress to a paralyzing feeling accompanied by crippling muscular stress or numbness.

When we have a serious fear of a thing or an animal, it is called a phobia.

A secondary emotion relating to fear is "nervousness." Tertiary emotions relating to nervousness are anxiety, dread, uneasiness, tenseness, apprehension, and worry. Another secondary emotion relating to fear is "horror." Tertiary emotions relating to "horror" include panic, shock, hysteria, terror, fright, and alarm.

Sadness

Sadness is an emotional pain that occurs in response to disappointment, grief, loss, sorrow, and helplessness.

It is a temporary state of melancholy and is a dominant emotion. Sadness is a natural and automatic emotion. But when it is extreme and persistent, it could be a symptom of depression.

Sadness is a normal emotion like fear or happiness. The death of a pet, the loss of a job or even breaking our favorite china could trigger sadness. When that feeling persists and overwhelms us permanently, it could be an indication of a mental health problem and a person experiencing such feelings should urgently seek professional help.

Surprise

Surprise is an emotion characterized by a sudden feeling of wonder or astonishment in response to an unexpected event or information. Surprises may be pleasant or unpleasant.

A secondary emotion relating to surprise is "surprise." Tertiary emotions relating to the secondary emotion of surprise are amazement, surprise, and astonishment.

Joy

Joy is a pleasant feeling of great pleasure and excitement. The emotional state of joy is characterized by feelings of contentment, happiness, gratification, satisfaction, and well-being.

Enthrallment

Tertiary emotions relating to the secondary emotion enthrallment are enthrallment and rapture.

Relief

A tertiary emotion you may feel relating to relief is also relief.

Anger

Anger is a strong feeling of displeasure, annoyance or hostility triggered by external provocation. Anger is associated with feelings of antagonism towards someone, something or an idea. Anger can be directed at oneself. When a person is angry at himself, the feeling of antagonism associated with his anger is directed at the person feeling the emotion.

While anger, like sadness, is a natural and often automatic reaction. Anger causes increased blood pressure, heart rate, adrenaline and noradrenaline levels. Extreme anger can substantially impair judgment.

Although anger is a primary emotion, it often occurs as a secondary emotion because it is frequently preceded by a negative primary emotion.

Anger is sometimes used as a mechanism to distract oneself from negative emotions that are self-focused. This happens when people stimulate the emotion of anger, either consciously or not, so as to avoid feelings of pain or vulnerability.

Doing this takes their attention off themselves and their unpleasant state and directs it at a person, a thing or an idea. This is considered by the person to be a better state than the state of pain. Anger by itself often does not feel bad to the person feeling it. This is because anger is associated with feelings of justification, moral superiority and pride. This does not deal with the pain or suppress it. What has happened is a shift of attention from the pain to the 'forced' anger. Once the anger wears off, attention reverts to the pain.

Managing Negative Emotions

Many of us don't like feeling angry, frightened, or sad; we tend to have an adverse response to emotions we feel are negative. Many of us would prefer to stay optimistic and positive, feeling cheerful and joyful. In fact, many of us were probably raised to always look at the bright side, not get angry, and keep our chins up when we felt sad. Maybe you've even felt severely anxious and did your best to just calm down.   None of these things is bad, and of course you don't want to feel negative emotions. It's important to realize, though, that emotions are neither good nor bad; they just are. Some might feel negative, but they're really just part of the human experience. Moreover, sometimes an emotion (for example, anxiety) is merely symptomatic of a larger issue. Your brain could be trying to get you to recognize what's going on. Think of it as a fever indicating you have an infection somewhere in your body. Anxiety can mean you need to invest in some self-care.

Not wanting to deal with difficult emotions means that we have very unrealistic expectations of life. Rather than viewing them as negative, we can look at them as valuable. Our emotions can be telling and powerful; we need to understand and embrace them.

Life is sometimes challenging, but we shouldn't shy away from emotions just because they make us uncomfortable.

Negative Emotions

How can we embrace "negative" emotions and live a fulfilling life? Whether or not you want to admit it, emotions that make you feel bad or uncomfortable are there. Most people don't love feeling anger, despair, disappointment, disgust, frustration, guilt, sadness, and shame, but we all feel these things.

Paul Eckman, a psychologist who pioneered the study of emotions, asserted in the 1970s that there are six fundamental emotions:

Disgust

Fear

Happiness

Sadness

Surprise

You might notice that four of these are perceived as "negative" emotions.

Ten years later, psychologist Robert Plutchik elaborated on Eckman's fundamentals. Plutchik stayed that there were actually eight emotions:

Anger

Anticipation

Disgust

Fear

Joy

Sadness

Surprise

Trust

Both Eckman and Plutchik elaborated on their findings and included a range of emotions with varying intensities. The wheel of emotions showcases this spectrum.

Negative Emotions Aren't Actually Negative

It might be hard to believe, but the emotions we perceive as negative can actually be good for us for many reasons.

They're completely normal. At some point in our lives, we started to believe that "negative" emotions were bad. Of course, it's important to be present and live a life with gratitude but expecting joy 100% of the time is incredibly unrealistic. What's more, we should feel open to discussing the "negative" emotions, because they're completely natural. Everyone has them. If we qualify the undesirable emotions as "bad," it only makes us feel worse when we feel them. Emotions - the ones that make us feel good and the ones that make us feel not-so-good - are part of what it means to be human. They're normal, and they help us cope with life.

They're there for a reason. All emotions, even the "negative" ones, are purposeful. Throughout human evolution, emotions have allowed us to survive and be healthy. For example:

Guilt and shame help us adhere to our own moral codes.

Anger protects us by motivating change.

Fear signals danger

Sadness builds empathy and connectivity

We've needed all these emotions to survive the evolutionary process. They might not be fun to experience, but they're there for a reason. It's up to us to determine their purpose in our lives. "Negative" emotions urge us to progress and mature.

They alert us. Emotions can act as signals that something is amiss. If you're feeling off-track or disjointed, emotions can catch your attention to alert you. Chances are, you'll experience moderate emotions at first. Annoyance, irritability, and frustration can be your brain's way of trying to gently tell you that something isn't right.

If you ignore those, the alerts become more obvious, and you'll experience stronger emotions like anger or fear. Unfortunately, some of us can ignore these signals, too, and our brains are essentially forced to get more aggressive with the messages. Emotions start to snowball into things like depression and rage. It's so important to listen to our bodies and our minds.

They motivate us. Emotions can serve as catalysts for change. In some scenarios, we might not have taken action if it hadn't been for our feelings of anger. It can prompt you to take charge and speak up. Recognizing, embracing, and channeling our anger can be extremely powerful. Dr. Martin Luther King, Jr., told us, "The supreme task is to organize and unite people so that their anger becomes a transforming force." When you feel "negative" emotions, they can be the push you need to be productive and solve problems.

They allow us to let go. It's no secret that ignoring our emotions can lead to serious health issues. If we give ourselves permission to feel our emotions, especially the difficult ones, it means we can also let it go and move on with our lives. If we don't deal with the emotions, they'll fester; if we embrace the emotions, we can then release them. The goal is not to have these emotions stew inside you forever, and it's also not to embrace them to the point of drowning in them.

Some emotions are unpleasant, difficult, and painful, but embracing them is the only way you'll ever be able to let them go. A good cry is an appropriate analogy here. If you allow yourself to break down and have a cathartic cry, you'll feel lighter and less burdened once you've finished.

You'll live a fulfilling life. We've seen in various cultures and philosophies that light and dark complement one another.

Perhaps you've read motivational quotes about only being able to appreciate sunny days by experiencing the rainy ones. As cliché as that might be, the sentiment is spot-on. Seeking equilibrium, understanding interconnectivity, and appreciating complementary forces will help you live a life of balance. The opposite forces of emotions allow us to be fulfilled. It's important to truly feel a wide range of emotions.

They make us stronger. Think of "negative" emotions as germs. Once you've fought off a virus, your immune system strengthens, and you're more resilient the next time you get a cold. The more you deal with "negative" emotions, the tougher you become. The next time that emotion comes along, you're equipped to handle it.

You know how to best cope with it, and you recognize that it's temporary. By dealing with your emotions, you're building your coping skills as a sort of immune system. The more you exercise your coping skills, the stronger and more effective they become. You don't want to hide from your emotions; be ready to handle them when they come.

Turning the Negative into Positive

Remember, we don't want to erase "negative" emotions. It's beneficial, though, to make the experience positive by understanding the value and purpose. The RISE process can help you remember how to learn from emotions that are uncomfortable.

R - Recognize the emotion. Allow yourself to feel it. Don't just push it away. Don't let it take over, but be present in the emotion. Acknowledge it, then release it.

I - Identify your emotion's purpose. Is it an alert? Is it your brain's way of offering you protection? Is it designed to motivate you effect some change? Consider why you're experiencing this emotion.

S - Stop and check. Most of the time, our "negative" emotions are justified, but sometimes, they're misguided. Pause to consider if you have all the facts before embracing your anger at a family member. If you're feeling anxious, is it because there are things to legitimately worry about, or have you created a bad habit of worrying too much? If you're feeling disappointed by someone's actions, think about the role you play in the situation.

E - Establish a plan. It's time to figure out your action. It could be something like showing gratitude for the gift of fear and its purpose to keep you out of danger, or it could be something like channeling your frustration at work into speaking up for yourself. It's also perfectly okay to have your plan be to just feel the emotion.

Having said that, though, we know that many of us have difficulty handling emotions that cause us stress.

Managing difficult emotions can be a real challenge. They're inevitable, of course, and we all experience them at one time or another. When we attempt to avoid them, though - by ignoring them, diverting our attention, or stifling them - we actually get the opposite of the desired effect. This exacerbates the situation, and those emotions tend to magnify. It sounds counterintuitive but trying to avoid difficult emotions results in having to experience them even more intensely. We need to be careful not to have a perfectionist mindset when it comes to our emotions. It's unrealistic to expect that our emotions will always be positive, but it can also be very problematic. Self-compassion and patience are necessary if we're to accept that difficult emotions are completely normal and unavoidable. A healthy perspective includes remembering that we should always seek balance.

They're symptoms that supply clues to larger issues. It's important not to ignore the messages, because they provide us with valuable data. That relevant information can be used to help identify a larger issue, shift your priorities, make choices, and solve problems. Don't forget, though, your RISE process - particularly, the third step when you stop to determine if you have all the necessary and accurate information. If you do, then it benefits you to incorporate that into your choices. Highly successful and emotionally intelligent people don't try to erase emotion from their choice making; rather, they put emotions' value to work for them.

Managing your emotions, especially the difficult or challenging ones, is beneficial for your ability to perform your best. It also improves your general well-being and peace of mind. We can show ourselves compassion and patience, knowing that it's perfectly natural to experience difficult emotions. A practical and very valuable application is meditation. It's an effective way to handle stress and anxiety so you can face the challenging emotions with a clear head.

Self-Compassion

Self-care, both emotionally and mentally, begins with compassion for yourself. Most of us have inner critics that can be quite severe; we'd likely never speak to a close friend the way we speak to ourselves. During a challenging time, it's especially important to treat yourself with kindness and patience.

Research shows people who show themselves compassion are typically less lazy and weak. Additionally, they're more self-aware, honest with themselves, and well-equipped to effectively navigate transitions and stumbling blocks.

To incorporate self-compassion in your life, there are strategies you can utilize. Think about how you speak to yourself. Does the inner voice tell you you're not good enough? A lot of us speak to ourselves this way, even though we'd never think to be so harsh to our loved ones. Start taking note of the language you use when you speak negatively to yourself. Are you berating yourself for going through a tough time?

Emotional Intelligence

The best way to manage your own challenging emotions and understand the emotions of others is to build your emotional intelligence. You'll recall that there are five basic tenets of emotional intelligence and incorporating four of these elements can help you handle emotions that are uncomfortable or difficult. It begins with self-awareness; you must first know and understand your own emotions. You need to be able to recognize and accurately identify what it is you're feeling.

Self-regulation means you're using your skills and resources to manage your emotions so that you don't impulsively react without thinking. Empathy and compassion are required, and you must show yourself the kindness you would extend to a loved one in the same situation. Lastly, motivation is the inner drive you need to want to grow as a person. Without it, you'd lose sight of why you're even working on managing the emotions.

Mental and emotional resilience refers to your ability to cope during a critical situation and quickly return to a normal state. Resilience is the result of developing strategies to stay calm during chaos and move on.

We all face stressors every day, and some of us are able to withstand more than others. Persistent stress wreaks havoc on your sense of balance if you haven't built resilience. It encompasses mental, physical, and emotional adaptations and coping skills. If you're resilient, it means you're able to bounce back from adversity, stronger than before.

In 1973, the first resilience research was published. It explored, through epidemiology, the coping mechanisms that we now know are part of resilience. Researchers also developed instruments to examine systems that support resilience development.

Researchers have done extensive work exploring the underlying issues that result in the need for resilience. For example, poverty, mistreatment or abuse, and disastrous events can affect a person in ways that warrant coping mechanisms. There are some factors, such as family bonds, mentors, and school influence, that can contribute to ensuring that those coping mechanisms provide positive outcomes.

Resilience is a process, not a character trait. Research has found that resilience is the positive outcome when a person has the ability to interact with elements that will protect them from danger and promote General wellbeing. When a person encounters a detrimental situation, he or she can approach it in one of three ways:

Angry or volatile outburst

Numbness and inability to react

Upset over the change

Resilient people react in the third fashion. They become upset, make necessary changes, and cope. The other two choices tend to result in assuming the role of a victim; placing blame or avoiding coping strategies typically do not foster growth or promote well-being. The goal is to respond to a circumstance, rather than have an impulse reaction. This can be tricky, since "negative" emotions such as fear and anxiety tend to impede our ability to tackle issues.

Thoughtfully responding means you can put an end to whatever the crisis is, cope, and bounce back.

Positive Factors

Coping strategies tend to be successful when coupled with positive factors that facilitate resilience. For example, you might be in an emotionally safe space to cope because you have positive surroundings like family, community, or school.

Biological Relationships

Three foundations of resilience - self-concept, self-esteem, and selfconfidence - spawn from three specific nervous systems (central nervous system, autonomic nervous system, and somatic nervous system, respectively).

Resilience can be especially important if you experience multiple crises. It takes a toll on the human body; chronic anxiety and constant worrying will diminish your body's immune system, making your susceptible to illness.

Resilience to stress has a neurobiological foundation. Your brain responds to elevated cortisol levels (brought on by stress) and decreases sympathetic nervous system activity. Resilience, which is a positive adaptation, plays a role in your long-term health and well-being.

Bouncing Back

We all face hardships and adversities in life. Resilience means that you don't allow those circumstances to define you or defeat you. Setbacks and failures can knock you down, but it's important to come back just as strong. Resilience is a part of emotional intelligence; some of the factors include:

Emotional regulation

Optimism

Positive attitude

Viewing setbacks as opportunities

If you're resilient, it means you learn from mistakes and failures, and you value those lessons. Remaining optimistic helps your mind and body cope with a disturbing experience. This means you're able to access all of your valuable cognitive resources, making it much easier to calmly analyze what has happened and consider a path for moving forward. Remember, resilience is not a character trait; it's an active process that requires determination and dedication. The payoff, though, is achieving goals even after unfortunate things have happened.

The goal is not to avoid or reject pain and disappointment; rather, resilience allows us to get through it without having it take over. It can be difficult to persist after trauma or misfortune. Are you resilient? There are some questions you should ask yourself. Do you solely blame yourself and your inadequacies for setbacks in your life? Do you demand and expect perfection from yourself at all times? A resilient person realizes that sometimes there are contributing factors, and life has ups and downs.

Setbacks Make Us Stronger

Crises can be overcome, and we can come out stronger on the other side. Failure - as much as list of us dislike that word - is natural. It's a part of every human's life. It's important to remember, though, that introspection, learning, and transcendence are also natural. Failure isn't a brick wall; it's a stumbling block.

Learning lessons from our failures is how we grow to be humble, mature, and empathetic. You might have the urge to harshly judge yourself, but resist it. You're developing your self-regulation, and your emotional intelligence will improve because of it.

Anxiety

Anxiety is one of the common secondary emotions; it is usually experienced in the place of another emotion which a person cannot adequately feel or even express. Anxiety may be a secondary emotion to anger. In itself, anxiety is a normal and sometimes healthy emotion which we experience when we are faced with what we consider a difficult or challenging situation.

It is also a natural response to stress; it is usually triggered as a result of fear or apprehension. But, anxiety can become a medical disorder when it becomes overwhelming and starts interfering with our daily activities. When feelings of anxiety become extreme and last well beyond six months, they become anxiety disorder.

Anxiety disorders are usually categorized by excessive worry, fear, and nervousness. Anxiety could alter how you process your emotions and behave in reaction to these emotions. Anxiety may be mild or extreme. Mild anxiety is the type which leaves you feeling slightly unsettled while extreme cases of anxiety usually have a largely adverse effect on your day-to-day living.

There is a difference between normal anxiety and anxiety disorders. As humans, anxiety is a normal emotion we experience when we face potentially harmful situations because it is necessary for our evolution and survival. When humans face potential danger, certain bodily alarms are set off in the body to alert us and trigger an evasive reaction. These alarms come in form of increased heartbeat, sweating, trembling, and heightened sensitivity to the surroundings.

The cause of this is the trigger of a hormone called adrenaline. When we sense danger, our body releases a rush of adrenaline which activates certain anxious responses in what has been termed the "fight-or-flight" response. The fight-or-flight response makes us to either or runs from a dangerous situation. While the fight-or-flight response was engineered back when humans were still quite primitive, it has definitely evolved into more contemporary things.

Feelings of anxiety are now being triggered by work, family, lifestyle, money, and other crucial things that command our attention and sets off adrenaline without actually requiring the fight-or-flight response. Those nervous feelings we get in a difficult situation or right before an important event mirrors the original fight-or-flight reaction. For example, when you get anxious about walking the streets at night, you will instinctively try to avoid possible danger if you do walk the street at night.

Ordinary anxiety serves as motivation to us and increases our chances of survival in our environment but anxiety moves beyond normal to a medical disorder when it becomes unnecessarily delayed or extremely severe or when it goes out of proportion to the anxiety trigger. Anxiety may manifest in the form of physical symptoms such as increased blood level, nausea, and so on, and all of these could be really damaging to our wellbeing.

Causes Of Anxiety

Over the years, there has been many research conducted to identify the underlying cause of anxiety but the cause of anxiety remains largely unknown. But, there are certain factors that could serve as triggers for anxiety. In fact, anxiety may occur as a result of the combination of two or more of these factors. Certain events, emotions, and experiences may also serve as triggers for feelings of anxiety or complicate them.

People have individual anxiety triggers but there are triggers that are common among the majority of the anxious population. There are also people who experience anxiety attacks without any trigger at all. To control your anxiety, you must identify what serves as a trigger for it. Identifying the factors and triggers that encourage feelings of anxiety in you is key to managing anxiety. In truth, you cannot actually manage anxiety, but you can manage the triggers so the anxiety becomes reduced or mild.

According to research, anxiety may be a genetic inheritance. Having a close family member with anxiety problems increases an individual's chances of experiencing anxiety issues. However, there have been no solid or substantial proof to discern whether anxiety inherited genetically is the result of certain genetic factors or the result of learning and adapting from our parents or primary caretakers.

A difficult childhood experience may serve as trigger for anxiety; this is even one of the most common triggers identified by experts. If you had a traumatic and highly stressful childhood growing up, there is the likelihood that you will develop huge anxiety problems as an adult. Emotional abuse, neglect, grief, physical abuse, social isolation, and bullying are some of the childhood experiences which can become triggers for anxiety.

For instance, a person who was raised by emotionally inconsistent parents is likely to develop problems of anxiety.

Separation anxiety is something that actually occurs when a child is separated from a primary caregiver from a very young age; it could be mild or acute, causing huge emotional trauma for the child.

Anxiety problems may also be triggered by certain health issues. When health issues serve as triggers for anxiety the result is usually very powerful due to the immediate feelings it stimulates. One of the health issues which could be a trigger for anxiety is any problem related to the heat. In fact, experts say that individuals with a generalized anxiety disorder are more prone to heart attacks and other heart diseases than other people.

A chronic health issue such as cancer could be the trigger for your anxiety. Living with a life-threatening health condition can be really disheartening, especially if it is one that has gone beyond a cure. It puts you in a constant state of fear, distress, worry, and apprehension about what is to come or what the future holds; this serves as a trigger for anxiety or anxiety attacks.

Diabetes, hyperthyroidism, asthma, chronic obtrusive pulmonary disease, and chronic pains are some of the other health problems which could trigger symptoms of anxiety. The best way to tackle anxiety caused by health issues is to become proactive and very aware of your situation. You may also reach out to a therapist to help manage the emotions being evoked by the results of your diagnosis.

Certain medications and over-the-counter prescriptions can also trigger feelings of anxiety. Sometimes, anxiety arise as a side-effect to the use of these medications. This is due to the fact that some ingredients in these medications give you feelings of unease or being unwell; they make you queasy. When you have these unsettling feelings of unease, another series of events may be triggered in your mind or body, resulting in more symptoms of anxiety.

Medications such as cough medications, weight loss pills, and birth control pills trigger symptoms of anxiety. Recreational and psychiatric medications may also trigger anxiety problems. If you do not have close relatives with anxiety or never experienced trauma or emotional/physical abuse as a child, then the cause of your anxiety may be a certain medication you are taking.

You probably love caffeine so much but do you even know it could be the source of your anxiety problem? Many of like to start our day with a cup of pleasant coffee; it can be refreshing. However, a study conducted in 2010 has revealed that caffeine has some anxiety-inducing effects which people with panic disorder (a form of anxiety disorder) are especially susceptible to.

Caffeine is a stimulant; it has the same effect on your mind and body that a frightening situation would. When you consume caffeine, it stimulates the fight or flight response which could heighten your anxiety and trigger an anxiety attack. Too many cups of caffeine will leave you feeling moody, jittery, nervous, and sleepless and all of these could definitely worsen your anxiety symptoms. Some foods and drinks can also trigger or worsen symptoms of anxiety. An example is sugar and alcoholic drinks.

You probably didn't know this but cutting back on food consumption could trigger anxiety problems. When you skip meals, your blood sugar level drops and this results in a rumbling tummy and jittery and sweaty hands. It is a necessity for you to eat balanced meals appropriately. Eating gives you much needed energy and nutrients with which you keep your body and mind healthy and functioning.

If you are the type who is too busy to eat three times a day like you should, then ensure you have a variety of healthy snacks at hand to make up for the lost meals. This will help prevent low blood sugar, nervousness, and anxiety symptoms. Also, keep it in mind that certain foods may affect your mood positively or negatively. Just like the pioneer of cognitive theories of emotions suggested, our thoughts have a large and unwavering impact on our emotional and physical state. The mind is the anchor of the body and this reflects with people who have anxiety problems. For instance, your choice of thoughts or words when you are scared, frustrated, or angry may trigger feelings of anxiety even when you don't expect it.

If you are the type who employs the use of negative words and thinking in your perception of yourself, it can largely trigger some primary emotions which aggravate anxiety. For instance, if you have a very important test coming up and your first choice of words to yourself is "Oh, there's no way I'll pass this test," your mind accepts this as an affirmation that you cannot pass the test. Then, feelings of stress, worry, and helplessness set in to further increase your physiological anxiety reactions.

Some risk factors increases a person's chance of developing anxiety symptoms. Apart from trauma, grief, or abuse, some other risk factors which could trigger symptoms of anxiety are stress, stress buildup, personality disorders, etc. For instance, some problems in your life and seemingly difficult situations may result in the buildup of stress which in turn causes anxiety symptoms to be triggered. Some of these problems include financial problems, overworking, unemployment, undue pressure, etc. There are also other stressors we continually experience in our daily life.

Anger as a trigger for Anxiety

Like we said, anxiety is usually experienced as a secondary emotion. So, which major primary emotion could be a trigger for anxiety? The answer is anger! Yes, you definitely didn't expect that answer since most people who have anxiety problems tend to be kind, polite, and vey self-critical; chronic worriers obviously don't seem like the type to get angry. Well, the keyword here is "obviously" which explains how we all seem to miss the fact anger could be a trigger for anxiety.

Often, anxicty is associated with fear and fear is regarded as the polar opposite of anger. What you may not know however is that fear is sometimes a trigger of anger which may further become a source of anxiety. Some people get angry because they feel weak expressing feelings of worries or concerns so they resort to covering this up with anger.

For others, anger is a core symptom of underlying anxiety problems and anger-anxiety is usually linked to the fight or flight reaction that occurs when we face a difficult situation. There are people who experience severe anxiety due to episodic anger, the fear of losing control, and the stress that comes with having to bottle anger in.

Firstly, anger is a very strong emotion which can induce great health consequences. How does anger even trigger anxiety? Anger serves as trigger to anxiety when it is bottled in rather than being let out through a healthy avenue. This problem starts from as early as childhood and is encouraged by the society. From a young age, we are taught that anger is a bad thing; it is rude, impolite, and should never be expressed because it makes us go out of control.

This of course results in anger denial as adults. Due to the many beliefs we have been fed about anger as kids, we tend to repress this emotion rather than express it. However, when you deny or repress a feeling, this feeling doesn't necessarily go away; instead, it is channeled towards another place. Acting like you are unoffended when someone upsets you doesn't make your anger go away, it is akin to setting off a time bomb.

The fact that we are made to believe that feelings that give us no pleasure are not meant to be acknowledged or expressed can cause even bigger problems such as feelings of shame, low self-esteem, and confusion. In time, we may learn to accept the cause of our anger as being normal instead of refuting or fighting against it. For instance, if as a child, you were bullied by an older person but you have been taught never to express your anger; your mind becomes conditioned to bottle anger in rather than express it.

When the fight or flight response is activated without any seeming danger or risk, it could result in a series of complex anger-related emotions which further heighten the level of anxiety. These include;

Irritation: Anxiety as an emotion makes a person susceptible to annoyance and irritation which happen to be some of the foremost negative triggers of anger. People who are constantly irritated usually feel bothered by company and they tend to react with anger. They may also become upset by their anxiety in general and choose to make an anger an outlet for their frustration.

Loss of control: Sometimes, anger is a person's natural response to situations where they feel like they aren't in control. Anxiety may make a person feel as though they have no form of control over some situations; this is quite common among people who experience anxiety attacks

Conclusively, as much as we understand that anger may be a symptom of anxiety, we must also recognize the fact that it could also be a major cause or trigger for anxiety. People with anger problems tend to especially feel high levels of stress which further leads to more stress and anxiety. Sometimes, when not effectively checked, anger and anxiety can become a cycle you become trapped in.

So, how you can you control your anxiety by mastering emotions such as anger and fear which are the primary emotional triggers? Let's find out!

How to Overcome Stress

Fear is a good thing as it keeps us alive, but fear and stress that you encounter while building your self-confidence is not something good, and we should strive to overcome them. Fear and stress are enemies of self-confidence. It is natural to experience fear and stress when you are trying out something new — conquering both places you on the path of success.

Self-confidence and Fear

Feeling afraid before attempting something new is normal, but experiencing fear in a detrimental way and in places where it is not required is a problem. It is perfectly normal to fear a leopard, but when you fear people of the opposite sex or talking to strangers, then that fear is not normal. Why do we have a fear of attaining self-confidence?

- Past experiences- A good example is a child who had a bad experience in his or her life. If a child was socially withdrawn, then he or she might experience irrational fear and prevent him or her from becoming self-confidence.

- False beliefs- False beliefs are responsible for the lack of confidence in self. These false beliefs will give you irrational fear, not to reason or question your belief.

- Parenting Style- Children can learn to fear by observing their parent's fears. We are aware that self-confidence can be learned during childhood, and so does fear.

These fears are deeply rooted in our genetic makeup, and they affect our efforts to build our self-confidence.

Self-confidence and Stress

I can guarantee you that if you have low or no self-confidence, you are likely to experience stress in our life. We can handle the stress of this life by becoming more self-confidence. If you learn to value and appreciate yourself, you get the ability to handle stress. It is important to be confident of avoiding stress. The journey to attaining your self-confidence is not an easy one, and you are likely to experience stress along the way. It might lead you to give up along the way and abandon the course of self-confidence.

How to Overcome Stress and Fear that Limit Self-confidence Learn to utilize the word 'NO'

If you have no time to do what your family or friends are requesting, it is okay to say no. If you also notice they are taking advantage of your kindness, put a stop to it and let them know that you will help them but not at the expense of your goals. When you are a people- pleaser, you get stressed as you are always doing stuff for other people and lacking time to concentrate on your stuff. Saying no will not make them think less of you, and they will not take it personally; therefore, be firm with your answer and take the wheel of your life back.

Slow down time

It is a situation where you are in an argument, and you are yelling at each other with the other person, it is okay to step out for a while. When you notice the situation is uncontrollable, take a deep breath and stop. Breath in deeply and exhale slowly. This act might look simple, but it will cool the heat. It will give you a chance to take things back to normal. Do not let the pressure and stress of a situation lower your self-confidence.

You are not a superhero

It is good to know when to stop. You should know that other people's problems are not yours. You might think that by getting involved too much, you are helping them. If you can be honest with yourself, you know you are not helping them. Take a step back and concentrate on our problems. We all have our problems in this life and carrying your burden as well as those of your friends can be overwhelming and only add to your stress.

Acknowledge that your memory is not accurate

Our brain is the library of all the information in our lives based on our beliefs, values, and perceptions. Most of the time, our memory is bias. You should know that everything in your memory does not represent facts.

For instance, if an event occurred and everybody in that even was asked to recollect what happened, you will have as many versions as the people present. To build your self-confidence, accept that your memory is not 100% accurate. Look at all the self-limiting beliefs in your library and reverse your perspective. It could be a lie that you have told yourself over and over again until it became a belief in your life.

Positive self-talk

You are the best solution to building your self-confidence. In everyday activities, we encounter things that push us to think we cannot make it. They stress you, and you think that the only option available is to give up. Boost your self-confidence by talking to yourself. Does it sound absurd? It is okay; just try it and notice how effective it is.

These small self-talks will improve your memory, build your self-respect, help you to manage stress, and boost your self-esteem. Remember, these benefits are based on the self-talk you are giving yourself. When you speak positively to yourself, you will boost your confidence, and when you speak negatively to yourself, the results will be negative.

Positive mindset

Human beings have a natural negative prejudice that secures us from danger. It is important for our safety, but it keeps us from exploring and implementing new ideas. The negative prejudice will affect your selfassurance. To overcome it, look for the positivity in every negative situation. Most positive things do not stick for a long while; on the other hand, the negative ones stick and grow roots. Reverse the negative thoughts by always having a minimum of five positive ones.

Keep the positive thoughts in your mind and let them sleep for a little longer than always. It is also important to recognize your bad feelings as well as good ones. Most of the time, we suppress negative thoughts instead of addressing them. It would be advisable to address them even if it is not the easiest thing to do. When you address the negative thoughts, you deny them a chance to stick to your thoughts and create an abode there.

Get rid of self-doubt

Self-doubt and victim mentality hinders your growth personally and professionally. Have you ever kept away from something because you think you are not qualified or because you think you do not deserve it? All this is doubt lodged in your mind. You are the only hindrance to your success and growth.

Evaluate your life and find the areas you have self-doubt. Dig out the roots and at the same time, work on yourself. When you doubt every little thing in your life, you will never take a step to do anything. You will always be stagnant, and prestigious opportunities will always pass you without noticing.

Become curious

Curiosity is only detrimental to cats after all curiosity killed the cat. To human beings, curiosity is important if you want to be successful and to gain confidence in yourself. When you are curious, you become observant and open to learning new experiences. A curious person is open to development and growth. Ask questions to get more insight. It will open new possibilities in your life, and at the same time, you will gain more confidence in yourself.

Embrace the fear

You should learn that fear is a gift. Fear brings stress and pain, and through them, we can create depth in life. Without fear, we live a superficial life. The fear you feel before engaging in something new can show you your capability to grow. When you feel fear and apprehension, you can approach it with curiosity or gratitude.

Beware of your instinctive reaction.

Fear can make us freeze, flight, or fight. These are the standard reactions of human beings. We react this way because we listen and follow our instincts. That is not where the problem lies, but allowing fear to dictate all your choices is the problem. Be cautious of your reactions as fear can stop you from growing out of your shell.

Treat all situations as if they are your choice

In this world, we encounter different situations every day. These situations that arise are not what we had planned for or what we want in our lives. It is always good to be ready for any outcome in life and at the same time, be ready to accept it as if it was of your choosing. There is no better way to handle it with love for you and others. Accepting the situation bypasses the emotional resistance as well as fear.

Be resourceful

When I say you should be resourceful, I am in no way telling you that you have to be wealthy or rich. It means that you should be creative and utilize what you have at hand. Use your creativity to solve problems from a neutral ground.

Be grateful for criticism

Keep in mind that when you are pushing forward for growth and to indulge in something new, people will always shoot you down. What do you do in such situations? Do you believe in their words? Do you give up? Trying out something new brings shame and fear to many people. Remember, the more the criticism, the more the success in waiting. Accept the criticism and be grateful for it. Never bow down to the pressures that accompany criticism.

Use the fear of failure to succeed

We all fear to fail, but our actions towards the said fear determine the difference in our success levels. You should not take the fear of failure as an outright failure. Use your failure to push you to achieve your goals and to succeed.

Take control of your thoughts

How do you react when something bad happens to you? Most of us relate bad things to themselves. If you put so much effort into achieving something, but it does not succeed, it does not mean that you are a failure, and neither does it mean that you did not put much effort into achieving it. Most of the time, the failure has nothing to do with you. Never personalize or over-analyze it.

Instead of sticking in one point blaming yourself, you should think of the next goal to work on. Success has many paths, and you have to try without giving up until you get your breakthrough. Even so, control your thoughts and never allow them to control you.

What is your automatic response to fear?

Be observant and know your initial reaction to fear. You should be aware that those responses are not hurting you only, but also, other people are affected directly or indirectly. It is not easy, and we often lie to ourselves that that is how we are created. It is important to know all our positive and negative characteristics. By doing so without judging ourselves, we give ourselves a chance to grow and change. Knowing all your aspects gives you a choice to use power to overcome your fear.

There is always calm at the center of a storm

Despite all your fears, there is self-confidence lodged inside of you. You should find out and make it your abode. In that place, you get the ability to commit to your long-term goals. Without self-confidence, you can only commit to short-term goals because you do not believe in your ability to see it through.

Get rid of your mediocre behaviors

You should know that most people without self-confidence use short cuts and mediocre behaviors. Did you know that people with self-confidence have worked hard to attain it, they were not necessarily born with it? You can pinpoint a confident person with the way he or she think, speak, walk, and carry himself or herself generally.

Self-confidence is nurtured to health and growth. It doesn't matter where you come from or who brought you up; these skills are cultivated. You need to train for self-confidence deliberately. If you want to have self-confidence, you need to mirror your actions on others who have succeeded in acquiring it. Trade your old and backward actions with those of a self-confident person. Take self-confidence as a duty or responsibility.

Act while in the state of fear

It is never wise to wait for fear to subside to act. As we said earlier, it is okay to fear, as it is only natural for every human being. Use your fear to push you to get what you want. Use it to fuel your self-confidence. The best way to conquer something that you fear to do is to do it. When you act in your state of fear, it makes you feel better, and you train yourself to fight it.

Don't avoid problems; seek them

Problems are meant to challenge you, grow from them, and learn a lesson from them. People with no self-confidence avoid problems while those with self-confidence look for them to give solutions. When you avoid problems you ruin your reputation as you did not complete your task but instead left it for someone else, you ruin your integrity, you get anxious and afraid, and you lack peace.

On the other hand, when you seek problems, you build your reputation as a problem-solver, and you get respected and admired. We often struggle with self-confidence because we have convinced ourselves that we cannot do it.

We have tried working things out to have good relationships, we have tried keeping fit, but all seem always to fail. If in your workstation you find people cannot trust you, you need to change and always stand with your word. If you promise to do something, you must do it always.

The bottom line to stick with is always to seek out problems. Failing in one project does not mean you give up. You should learn what you did wrong and where you made your miscalculations correct them and try again until you succeed. Exercise builds your self-confidence.

In self-confidence, the majority never win

In today's world, most people are not self-confident. Most of them are full of insecurities. Their concern is on what people will say about them and always act to please. Avoid following what most people are doing to avoid fear, anxiety, and insecurities. To eliminate fear, chose the people to emulate carefully.

You should also note that the loudest people are mostly wrong role models. They talk a lot to hide their insecurities and fears. When looking for someone to emulate, look for a person with the qualities you want. If you want to grow your self-confidence; therefore, it is only natural to look for someone full of self-confidence and who understands their value.

What doesn't increase you takes from you

Look at your lifestyle, is it filled with positivity, healing, and support, or is it full of negativity that keeps you from growing? Most of us have negative influences that weigh us down, such as the media, people, environment, and our behaviors. These influences keep us from becoming a better version of ourselves.

Train yourself to cut them from your life. Look at what is not helping you and cut it from your life. You should note that all the things that are not helping you are most likely hurting you. Also, look at the company you are keeping. If they are people full of negativity, do not expect to reap positivity from them.

Relax

Stress is a major factor that hinders the growth of our self-esteem. You will encounter many things in this life, and most of them are not pleasant. Your responsibilities will overwhelm you, and different things in this life will stress you. Take time out and find something that will help you to relax. You can go for a swim, take a hot bath, or even find a game to indulge in. Find whatever works for you and relax as you enjoy.

Set goals

At the beginning of each day you must know what you would want to achieve. Set realistic goals and keep track of their progress by having a list of all you have accomplished. It will make you feel a sense of accomplishment when you find yourself striking off all the things you have achieved. You will find that some days you will not strike as many accomplishments as others, but the trick is always to strive to be better every day.

Help out

I do not have double standards. I know I asked you to step aside and know that you are not a superhero. I still stand with the previous statement, but in some situations, helping a person in need and seeing results helps to boost your self-confidence a lot.

As you are helping, make sure you can notice results and do not let their problems stress you. One selfless act can do amazing things to your self-confidence.

Take a different viewpoint

Sometimes we allow one angle of view to affect our confidence. It is good to always think outside the box. Try doing this differently from the normal. Look at situations more realistically, and you will realize it is possible to achieve what you previously thought was impossible. Have a different mindset always to want to try instead of giving up based on the phase value. By looking at things from a different perspective, you will get rid of negative thoughts and inject positivity as the default setting in your life. You will eventually become a go-getter.

Try new ideas

You have no idea how our brains love to learn new stuff. We all need a creative channel; games, dance, art, crocheting, or cooking. We the current technology it is easier to get either of the above creativities. All you need is to log on YouTube and watch some videos. Remember, you are a click away from so many new ideas.

Overcoming Negative Feelings with Cognitive Therapy

Emotions are viewed as 'lower level' reactions. They initially happen in the subcortical regions of the cerebrum, for example, the amygdala and the ventromedial prefrontal cortices. These territories are answerable for creating biochemical responses that directly affect your physical state.

Emotions are inserted into our DNA and are thought to have created as an approach to assist us with reacting rapidly to various natural dangers, much like our 'battle or flight' reaction. The amygdala has additionally been appeared to assume a job in the arrival of synapses that are basic for memory, which is the reason enthusiastic recollections are regularly more grounded and simpler to review.

Emotions have a more grounded physical establishing than feelings meaning specialists discover them more straightforward to quantify equitably through physical signals, for example, bloodstream, pulse, cerebrum action, outward appearances, and non-verbal communication.

Feelings are viewed as going before emotions, which will, in general, be our responses to the various sensations we experience. Where feelings can have an increasingly summed up understanding over all people, emotions are more abstract. They are impacted by our encounters and elucidations of our reality, dependent on those encounters.

Feelings happen in the neocortical districts of the mind and are the subsequent stage by the way we react to our emotions as a person. Since they are so abstract, they can't be estimated the way feelings can.

Therapists have since a long time ago investigated the scope of human feelings and their definitions. Eckman (1999) recognized six starting essential feelings:

Happiness

Surprise

Fear

Sadness

Disgust

Anger

He later developed this to incorporate a further eleven necessary feelings:

Guilt

Relief

Shame

Sensory Pleasure

Excitement

Contempt

Embarrassment

Pride

Amusement

Contentment

Satisfaction

While we can utilize the name negative, with what we think about feelings, understand that all feelings are totally normal to encounter. They are a piece of our instilled DNA. What is increasingly significant is determining when and why negative feelings may emerge and creating positive exercises to address them.

Negative Emotions Instances

As we've investigated, negative feelings are ordinary. Without them, we wouldn't have the option to acknowledge positive ones. Simultaneously, if you discover you reliably have a propensity towards one specific feeling – particularly a negative one – it merits investigating why that may be. Here are more typical negative feelings and why they may emerge:

Anger

Ever have somebody tell you know no to accomplishing something you need? How does that make you feel? Does your blood start to heat up, your temperature rise, and do you figuratively 'see red'? This is ordinarily how outrage is portrayed. Your body is responding to things not going your way, and it's an attempt to correct that. Frequently when we're furious, we'll yell, our face will register our resentment, and we may even throw things around. We're attempting to get our way in a situation, and this is the primary way we think will work. In case you're regularly responding to situations along these lines, it's a smart thought to investigate why and concoct increasingly positive measures.

Annoyance

Do you have a partner who maybe talks too loudly? Does your partner consistently leave their messy dishes in the sink? Even though we may like our friends and love our partner, these exercises can make us feel really irritated. Alluding to Pluchik's wheel, you can see that disturbance is the weaker type of anger. While not as severe as an outrage, it's the aftereffect of a particular way of thinking – something has occurred, or somebody is doing something you wish they wouldn't. What's more, you have no power over it.

Fear

Fear is regularly referred to as one of the essential core feelings, and that is because it's intensely connected with our feeling of self-protection. It's a learned reaction to caution us about hazardous circumstances, surprising obstructions, or disappointments. We don't feel fear to feel bothered, unexpectedly, it's there to assist us with exploring a potential threat effectively. Grasping the feeling of fear and investigating why it emerges can help you with setting yourself up proactively to handle difficulties.

Anxiety

Much like anxiety, this looks to caution us about potential dangers and threats. It's frequently observed as a negative feeling as its seen as having an agitated attitude that disables our judgment and our capacity to act. A new study has discovered the opposite. Experts discovered having anxiety elevated member's capacity to perceive faces with irate or frightful demeanors. They measured the electrical power in the brain and found that non-clinically examined members moved their energy from tactile (communicating the feeling) to engine (physical activity) circuits. Mostly, members with anxiety were increasingly prepared to react and respond to apparent dangers.

Sadness

At the point when you miss a cutoff time, get an awful evaluation, or don't verify that activity you had your expectations stuck on, you'll most likely feel pathetic. Pity happens when we are disappointed with ourselves, our accomplishments, or the conduct of another person around us. Bitterness can be great to encounter as it shows to us we are enthusiastic about something. It tends to be an incredible impetus to seek after the change.

Guilt

Guilt is a perplexing feeling. We can feel this in connection to ourselves and past exercises that we wish hadn't occurred, yet additionally concerning how our conduct impacts everyone around us. Guilt is frequently alluded to as an 'ethical feeling' and can be another robust impetus to urge us to make changes throughout our life.

Apathy

Like guilt, this can be an unpredictable feeling. If you've lost energy, inspiration, or enthusiasm for the things you've recently appreciated, this could be identified with a lack of concern. Like outrage, it can emerge when we lose control over a situation or circumstance, yet as opposed to losing control, we seek after an increasingly inactive forceful delivery of resistance.

Despair

Ever attempted to accomplish a specific assignment or objective on various occasions and not succeeded? Did that make you want to throw your hands up, and stay in bed with an enormous tub of ice cream? That is despair, and it's a feeling that emerges when we aren't getting the outcomes we need. Depression gives us a reason to abandon our ideal objectives, and it yields to a self-protection strategy. Despair can be a valuable suggestion to take a break and regroup before proceeding to pursue a challenging goal.

The Cause Of Negative Emotions And Why We Have Them

When you start investigating negative feelings somewhat more, you can truly begin to perceive what may trigger or cause them, and why we have them at all.

As far as causes, it could be various things, for instance:

> Getting caught up in traffic (Anger)
>
> Break up in a relationship (Sadness)
>
> Inability to stick to a workout regime (Despair)
>
> Colleague forgetting to complete a task (Annoyance)

Feelings are a wellspring of data that help you comprehend what is happening around you. Negative emotions, specifically, can assist you in perceiving dangers and feeling organized enough to decidedly deal with potential threats.

A wide range of encounters in our lives will instigate diverse, passionate responses to contrasting degrees of power. As a person, you will encounter a full scope of feelings all through your life because of quickly evolving circumstances.

CBT Strategies For Eliminating Negative Thoughts

Find the issue and theorize solutions. Journaling and talking with your specialist can assist you in finding the base of your downturn. When you have a thought, record in a straightforward sentence precisely what's troubling you and consider approaches to improve the issue. A sign of depression is misery — a mistrust that things can ever show signs of improvement. Making a list of things you can do to improve a circumstance can help ease burdensome feelings. For instance, in case you're doing battling depression, things you could do may include joining a neighborhood club dependent on your inclinations or register for Internet dating.

Create affirmations to neutralize negative thoughts. In the wake of finding the root issues of your negative feelings, think about the negative thoughts you use to those positive ones. Compose a self-explanation to neutralize each negative idea. Keep in mind your self-affirmations and repeat them back to yourself when you see the little voice in your mind sneaking in to snuff out a positive idea. In time, you'll make new associations, replacing negative thoughts with positive ones.

Self- affirmations shouldn't be excessively a long way from the negative idea, or the psyche probably won't acknowledge it. For instance, if the negative idea is, "I'm so discouraged at present," instead of saying, "I'm feeling extremely cheerful now," a better explanation may be, "Each life has high points and low points, and mine does, as well."

The message shows you it's alright to bump up the level of happiness you are experiencing. Simultaneously, your psyche cheers itself for keeping happiness under wraps to shield itself from frustration. It's okay to perceive that part of you attempting to accomplish something substantial.

Some of the time, self-affirmations become too normal and should be revived. Specialists prescribe interpreting your self-affirmations into different dialects so you may exchange, or reword them, potentially, in any event, bumping up their upbeat feelings a bit. "For instance, the self-affirmation, "It's alright to investigate my ups" may turn into "It's alright to have a super 'up' day."

Figure out how to acknowledge disappointment as a typical part of life. Disappointing circumstances are a part of life, and your reaction can influence how rapidly you can push ahead.

Somebody experiencing a breakup may accuse themselves or even put on weight, thinking, "What's the point in looking great? I'll never meet any other person." A superior methodology may be to enable yourself to feel baffled and recollect that some things are out of your control. Work on what is inside your control: Write down what occurred, what you gained from the experience, and what you can do another way next time, looking out for excessively negative thoughts. This can assist you with proceeding onward and you can sleep comfortable thinking about your future.

Finish every day by envisioning its best parts. Toward the finish of every day, record or type into an online diary the things throughout your life you're generally appreciative of. Recording positive thoughts, and in any event, sharing those thoughts on the Web, can assist you with creating a new relationship in your mind or making new pathways. Somebody who's made another channel of reasoning may go from getting up in the first part of the day thinking, "Ugh, another workday" to "What an excellent day it is."

Find new chances to think positive thoughts. Individuals who go into a room and promptly think, "I despise the color of that wall," may instead prepare themselves to find five things in the room they feel emphatical about as quickly as would be prudent. Set your telephone to remind you three times each day to reframe your thoughts into something positive. Therapists suggest "buddying up" with another person chipping away at a similar procedure. That way, you and your friend can get energized over having positive thoughts and encounters to impart to one another for the day.

Strategies to Eliminate Stress

Identify the root of the stress

Finding the cause of why you are stressed is an important step that can help to eliminate stress. There are times when one feels stresses or one feels uncomfortable and thinks a lot about something, yet the person is not sure what the issue is. To get rid of stress, one should find what is causing you to be stressed up.

One should commit some 'alone time' and talk to oneself and find out why they are stressed out. To find what makes you stressed, you should ask yourself questions like; who is concerned in this? What did I do yesterday? Who was I with when this happened? Such questions help one identify the cause of the stress easily. Identifying what causes stress is the first step to eliminating stress.

Get rid of commitments that are not necessary

One should avoid getting committed to things that are not necessary. Depending on who you are and what you do, we all have different commitments. One may be committed to their children, their marriage partner, their work, their education, their spiritual knowledge and much more. It is important for a person to know what commitments are necessary and which are not.

One should only concentrate on things important to them. You might find a person putting so much effort into something that should be done by another person. You should let everyone play their role. It is through having all those commitments that are not necessary for your thoughts, that you find yourself stressed. The moment one gets rid of unnecessary commitments, one becomes focused and does not get stressed out. One should only be committed to necessary things.

Avoid postponing

Postponing should be avoided if one wants to get rid of stress. At times we say we will do things at a later time or at a later date mostly because we are lazy or because we have something else we are doing at the moment. Procrastination is the thief of time. One should do tasks and things immediately as they emerge to avoid having so many things to do at a particular time. When one postpones, you come to realize later that you have no time left and you have loads of work to do. This makes one stressed out thinking of how they will manage to be done perfectly and on time. A simpler solution to all this is to do things at the scheduled time. By this, you will always meet the timeline and will not be stressed out. One who wants to get rid of stress should do things at the scheduled time and avoid postponing anything.

Be organized

One should do things in an organized manner and in a neat way to avoid stress. At times we might plan things and everything falls into place, but there is that one time when we slide and try to squeeze in something else. This squeezing in may make us stressed out as there is no place for what we have squeezed in.

Disorganization may also stress out someone when you urgently need something but you cannot find it because you are not sure where it is. One might be looking for a certain certificate that is needed for a job interview and it is urgent, but you do not find it because you are disorganized. This will make you lose the chance to get the job and in turn, you become stressed. If the person was organized they would have known the certificate was in a certain drawer or bag and they can get it out and they get a chance to get the job. One who wants to avoid stress should not be disorganized but should plan everything in an organized manner.

Do not be late

One who wants to be stress-free should always do things on time. When one is behind his/her schedule, one tends to be stressed up. We should try as much as we can to be punctual enough so as to start things on time and finish on time. When one is late when doing something, you always feel stressed out. When you have an exam at 8 and you are not in the exam room by 8 you get stressed.

One thinks of the many possibilities that could happen if they missed the chance. If you are late you will have to redo the exam. This will make you stressed and you will start blaming yourself for not being punctual enough. If you are late to go to the bus station and the bus leaves before you are there, you will have to get other means of traveling. This makes you stressed out while searching for another means of transport. One should try as much as possible to always be punctual and do things at the right time.

Do not control others or things

If you do not want to get stressed out, do not control things or other people. We do not have the power to do that and whenever we force ourselves to do so, we get stressed because things might not really turn out as we expect. One might think that if you control a person and tell them to do a certain job for you, it will make it easier for you.

The person may or may not do the job, as whatever they do is under their control not yours. If they decide not to do what you had told them, you will have to do the job. Doing the job means you will have to fix that at a particular time, which means you will have to do it in a hurry. You can only give directions and controls to yourself.

A person of sound mind will do what they want regardless of whether it is right or wrong. You should just let things flow as planned but not as you wish. You should respect other people's choices and the way they control their things. One who wants to avoid stress does not control other people, but only controls himself/herself.

Avoid people who stress you out

To avoid stress, one should avoid people who stress him/her out. There are people who when we first meet we just feel stressed out. They can be our employers, teachers, parents, colleagues, relatives or even friends. One should avoid being in the presence of such people because they will always stress you out. If your employer stresses you out, try to avoid him/her. It can be that whenever your employer sees you in the wrong they remind you of a past event that stresses you out. An employer might see you trying to fix live wires and they start mocking you saying how the last time you tried doing that the firm lost a lot of property in a fire. Maybe whenever you remember that incident you get stressed out. One should avoid such people as they will only do you more harm than good. One who wants to avoid stress should avoid people that cause them to be stressed.

Appreciate everything and everyone in life

If you want to avoid stress, always appreciate everyone and everything life gives you. One should learn to show gratitude. Sometimes we stress out because things did not end up as we expected. Maybe you were doing an exam and you get a grade B while you were expecting to get an A. You should appreciate whatever life offers you.

When life gives you lemons, make a cocktail out of it. Do not ask for more. That is what you got and that is what is yours. You will not get another so you should just accept and strive to do better the next time. If you want to be associated with a particular group of people because you think they are cool, but you end up being in another group of people, appreciate them. You can still be happy with them if not happier. When we learn to appreciate what we have, we will not get stressed out.

Exercise and eat foods that are healthy

If you want to reduce stress, eat healthy foods and do a lot of exercises. Exercise rejuvenates our body and makes us stronger.

When you exercise your mood changes and you become happy. Exercise and eating healthy go hand in hand. There are foods that make one moody and there are foods that do not have mood effects on a person.

A healthy person is less prone to stress. Exercise does not leave room for stress in a person's body. Exercise also gives one some time for himself/herself. As you exercise, you think more about yourself and the situations you are in. This prevents one from getting stressed as they have a plan for their lives. Eating healthily and doing exercise regularly can help reduce stress.

Plan to do important things only

If you want to avoid stress, have a to-do-list of important things only. One should not put loads of jobs on their list. There are things that even if you do them, they will not impact on you. One should get rid of such activities. Concentrate on things and activities that are important and necessary. If you think something does not help you in any way get rid of it.

One who keeps a long to-do-list without caring whether it is helpful or not is prone to be stressed. This is because the person has each of their minutes planned for and whenever they try to fix some time for themselves in between they will mess things up. One should only strive to do things important to you and leave out other things. To avoid stress, one should create a to-do-list of important activities only.

Do what you like most

One who wants to reduce stress levels or get rid of it completely should exercise doing what they like doing most. We are all different and we have different preferences. Our talents, hobbies, and abilities are different. Different people may like doing different things like listening to music, taking a walk, going to the movies, skating, playing tennis, helping others, playing soccer, reading novels and books or even writing blogs.

One should put so much attention to what they like. The body wants what it wants. If you give the body what it wants, you will not become stressed out easily. People find their happiness from small things. I personally listen to music to find myself in a fantasy world. When you do what you like doing, you will spend most of your time being happy. One who wants to get rid of stress should spend their free time doing activities that they find fun.

Talk to someone

One who is stressed should find someone to talk to. The person can be a friend, a relative or anyone you trust. When you talk to someone you feel better. It is through talking to someone that you get to exchange thoughts. When you talk to someone the person gives his/her ideas and thoughts on a particular issue. The thoughts of the person can help you get a new perspective to a new thing.

When you talk to someone you feel you have gotten something off your chest. It is important to talk to someone when stressed out. Talking to another person when stressed prevents depression. To avoid stress one should reach out and talk to someone about the issue at hand.

Be assertive

One who wants to eliminate stress should always mean what they say. When one says yes, they should mean their yes and when they say no they should mean their no. One should not be influenced by others to do things or not to do things. You might do things because you were influenced by someone then when the consequences come to be you regret alone and be stressed out.

Everything has its own consequences. One should, therefore, make assertive choices after critical thinking. One should not do something because his/her friends have done it but should do what is right. The right thing is usually hard to do but we should strive to do it. The simpler thing is mostly the wrong thing. Wrong things have negative consequences which will get you stressed. To avoid stress, one should mean and do what they say.

Take caffeine in regular amounts

Caffeine should be taken in the correct amounts by someone who wants to get rid of stress. Caffeine is a stimulant. It is found in a drink like tea and coffee. One should take such drinks in regular amounts as they contain caffeine which increases anxiety levels. People are different and each person has a maximum caffeine intake. One should try not to exceed it as it will increase anxiety and stress levels.

Stress should be avoided and in case one gets stressed they should try to eliminate it. There are many ways in which one can avoid stress. One should avoid situations and people that make him/her stressed. One should avoid commitments that are not necessary. One should not postpone things and should always do things at the scheduled time.

One should always be organized and never be late to do anything. One should not give himself/herself the mandate to control another person or thing. One should have a simple to-do-list that is made up of important things only. One who wants to get rid of stress should exercise and eat healthy foods. One should use their free time to do what they like doing most.

One should have a regular caffeine intake depending on their threshold. One should exercise gratitude and appreciate others and whatever they get to have in life. One should always be assertive and always strive to do the right thing. One should talk to someone if they feel stressed out. There are many ways of eliminating stress. Above are just a few.

Strategies to Eliminate Our Fears

Know what your fears are

One who wants to eliminate their fears should start knowing what his/her fears are. We all have different fears. Each person has his/her own fear. One can fear height, water, darkness, spiders, being alone or flying just to name a few.

When one realizes that they fear a particular thing or person, they should accept that they fear those things. After one has accepted, they should not try to hide from them. If you fear something, you should realize that it will never end. If you fear darkness, there is no time that will come for darkness to cease to exist.

Knowledge is power. When you have the knowledge of your fears, you will not find yourself in hard situations when faced with your fears. Knowing your fears should be the first step taken by one who wants to get rid of their fears.

Learn to appreciate

One who wants to overcome fear should learn how to show gratitude. When you learn to be appreciative of things you have and situations you are in, you will get rid of fear. If you fear flying on a plane, be appreciative that you got the chance to fly in a plane. If you fear to lose a job, appreciate that you currently are doing the job and you have not lost the job.

When you learn to show gratitude when faced with your fears, you will view the positive side and you will have fewer emotions connected to the fear. When you show gratitude to someone or something, you feel good. It is good to appreciate something if it is nice. One who wants to eliminate stress should exercise the act of gratitude.

Discover what emotions are associated with fear

One who wants to eliminate fear should identify the feeling or emotion connected to the fear they have. One might have different feelings or thoughts for different fears. You might feel shocked when you see a spider, you might feel anxious when flying on a plane and you do not know when you will get down, you might feel sad when you think of losing your job and when you think of everything that will happen when you lose the job.

Mostly when someone thinks of their fear they start to overthink and they get different emotions while thinking. You might be having the fear of failing an exam and when you think about it you feel pitiful for yourself, then you remember how much your parents have struggled to see you in school you start hating yourself and have many more feelings. These are the reasons why one should identify the emotions and feelings they get when they face their fears.

Write them down

One who wants to get over their fears should write them down. Most times thinking about our fears only gets us more stressed. At times it makes us even more stressed than we were before. It is therefore wise for someone to list write their fears down if they want to get rid of them. When you write them down, you feel better and you feel relieved just a little bit.

Writing helps us to express what is in our thoughts and what we feel. When writing, one should not be restricted to a particular concern but should list all that is on their mind. One can even go further and start drawing what they think they feel or have in their chest associated with that fear. One who wants to get rid of their fears should write them down.

Talk to someone

Talking to someone about your fears will help you eliminate your fears. One might have had a fear of flying and they decide to talk to someone. When talking to the person about your fear, they tell you that they have flown several times and it is fun and maybe you should try it out with them. This might help you get a better image of flying.

When you talk to a person about your fears and what you feel about your fears, the person tries as much as they can to change the situation. One might not necessarily change your perception towards your fear but they might help you know how to face it. They might give you stories or testimonies of people who have made it through and you encourage yourself and hope all will be well.

One should make sure that after talking to a person they should not leave the person the way they came in terms of facing and handling the fear. Talking to someone can be a great way of eliminating our fears.

Learn not to control things

To eliminate fear, one should not control situations or things. A person might think that because they are good at something they can never fail or make a slight mistake at it. We are humans and we can never be perfect. You might be a punctual employee always on time doing your tasks and compliant, but one day you might delay a bit and you will get your fear from that. You will not know how to face your employer because you have always told yourself you are the best and no one can beat you at being punctual. You start fearing that the employer might fire you or you start fearing the employer might bump you down in the hierarchy. We should not control things or people if we want to get rid of our fears.

Learn from others

One who wants to get rid of their fear should learn from others. There are many people who share a common fear. Some have managed to get through it while some are struggling to get over it. One who wants to eliminate their fears should reach out to such people. If someone already made it overcome the fear, find out what they did to overcome the fear.

If you find people who are still struggling to get over it, learn what they are doing. Every day should be a learning day to someone who wants to get rid of their fears. You should even try to associate yourselves with people who have the same fear as you have and are trying to overcome it. One may fear to break up with a spouse and when you go to your friends who have the same issue, they tell you what they do to always see they are together. To eliminate your fears, you should learn from other people who have or who had the same fear as you.

Pray or meditate

One who wants to get rid of their fears should pray and ask for help. Christians are taught that God listens and answers our prayers. There are times you struggle with something so much that you do not know what to do next. One who has reached this stage should try and seek help from a religious perspective.

Christians should ask God for help and Muslims should ask Allah to answer their prayers. This depends on the religious background of a person. I am a Christian and I personally believe whatever you ask shall be given unto you. If one is not religious or finds it hard to pray, one can meditate. Meditation is as good as praying and helps one to overcome their fears too. One should choose whatever they think will be effective for them. A person who wants to get rid of his/her fears should pray or meditate.

Accept that everyone makes mistakes

One who wants to get rid of his/her fears should understand that no one is perfect and we all make mistakes. Some of our fears are caused by failing. One might have the fear of failing a test, of not doing well at the place of work, of not emerging the best in a fashion show or of not meeting the sales of a particular item. We should, however, understand that we have all experienced points in our lives when we failed at a particular thing. One cannot always be successful at everything you do and if that happens you are not doing something right.

One should, therefore, understand that failure opens a road for success. When you fail chances are people will mock or laugh at you while others will hold your hand and show you the way to succeed. It is therefore up to us to decide how we emerge after a failure. We should not be defined by failure. One who wants to get rid of fear should not let failure put them down.

Let life be

One who wants to get rid of his/her fears should flow with the events of life. If you want to live life peacefully, just flow with the way things are. At times we create fears because of people's opinions about us and how they judge us. One fears to talk in front of a large crowd because you are afraid of the impression you have on people or because you are afraid people will talk about you. One should not let their fears be based on such small issues.

People will always speak their views and thoughts about something or someone and because we all have different preferences and we should not let that bother us. Maybe when you do something great some people will not notice because they are not destined for greatness. After all, people have talked about you before and life went on after that.

Even with our fears, we should just flow with life in case we face them. One might be at 45 years old and have a fear of losing his/her job and they eventually lose it. Being 45 years old that might not be the first job you have lost. After losing the first job life continued as usual. We do not know what life holds for each one of us. One who wants to get rid of his/her fear should just let life be and flow with everything as it happens.

There are many strategies one can use to eliminate his/her fears. One should start with identifying his/her fear and dig to know what emotions and feelings are associated with fear. Once one has known what emotions are connected with the fear, they should find a way to control the emotion or feeling. One should talk to someone about their fears or talk to trained personnel and if they find that hard they can write their thoughts about the fear down.

One should seek religious help by praying and if they find that hard they can meditate. One should understand that failure is not permanent and everyone at some point has failed in a particular thing. One should not create fears because they are afraid of peoples' opinions and thoughts. One should flow with life because even after everything happens life will go on. One should learn to appreciate the opportunities they have and not view them as fears.

Negative thoughts, stress, and fears are all things that can cause us to be mentally ill and depressed. They are concerned with our cognitive behavior and one should try to eliminate them as soon as they realize they have developed them. They can be hard to avoid and eliminate but one should try as much as they can to get rid of them.

There are strategies that apply to all three issues. Strategies, like talking to someone, writing them down, exercising and eating healthy and praying or meditating, can all help eliminate the issues. One who wants to eliminate negative thinking, stress or his/her fears should fight as much as they can since it is not easy. There are times when one gets halfway there and loses hope because they cannot see the fruits their efforts but that should not be a reason for them to stop. One who has made a personal choice to eliminate all this does not turn back.

Regular Mindfulness Exercise

Most of us live quite busy lives. Between jobs, school, housecleaning, shopping, social events, family obligations, and required time to eat and sleep we are nearly constantly doing something. During this daily rush that lasts one week after the next, we lose connection with ourselves and the present moment. You begin to lose track of your own mental state and how you are doing. For instance, you will rarely notice how you are feeling as you complete tasks, as you are focused on what you are doing and what you have to do next.

Thankfully, there are ways in which you can re-center yourself during the business and find yourself in the present moment. You can understand and accept yourself without judgment. This exercise is incredibly impressive, with a large number of scientific studies finding that it can reduce stress and increase a person's overall life happiness. Some other benefits of regularly practicing mindfulness include:

Increased Mental Health

Mindfulness is regularly used during the process of therapy in order to treat a number of conditions, struggles, and conflicts. Some of the situations that mindfulness can improve mental health include when used with depression, anxiety disorders, substance abuse, obsessive-compulsive disorder, couples therapy, eating disorders, bipolar disorder, and more.

Increased Physical Health

Surprisingly to many people, but well understood by therapists, is the power of mindfulness can increase a person's physical health, along with their mental health. For instance, regular use of this exercise may improve sleep, lower blood pressure, treat heart disease, improve gastrointestinal symptoms, and lessen chronic pain.

Increase Overall Well-Being

By using mindfulness regularly, you will learn how to increase selfcompassion, release judgment, calm the mind, and release stress. By regularly using this exercise in your daily life you will find you are more satisfied and can more fully and easily enjoy the pleasures of life as they occur.

You will have the ability to engage with others more fully in activities while also being more capable when dealing with difficult events. As mindfulness teaches people to focus on the present, it becomes easier to avoid getting caught on in stress, worries, and regrets. This then helps to increase your selfesteem and kindness, allowing you to know yourself better and you can connect more deeply with others.

There are many different mindfulness exercises you can use. Please, try multiple varieties and find what works best for you. Then, when you have time, you can decide which exercise to use depending upon the time available. Some exercises require as few as three minutes, whereas others might require ten or fifteen minutes.

If you are interested in practicing a basic form of mindfulness, try following these simple steps:

1.   Set aside some time in a quiet and calming environment. You don't needany special equipment, but it is best if you can sit or lay somewhere that you feel comfortable. It doesn't matter if this is on a bed, in a chair, on a cushion, or even sitting on the floor. Simply, find someplace where you can focus on yourself rather than sitting in an uncomfortable position or somewhere with outside distractions.

2.   Allow yourself to focus on the present moment. You don't have to worryabout keeping your mind empty or finding a deep state of inner calm. All you have to do is focus on the present moment without judgment. This may be difficult at first, but with a little exercise, you will be able to complete this easily.

Don't let any difficulties deter you, as this is a simple form of mindfulness and only requires a little exercise.

3.   It is normal for judgments to occur while you are focusing on the present.These judgments can be caused by your inner critic, or they may be focused on an outside source. Either way, make a mental note of the judgments, and then let them go and melt away.

4.   Your mind might get carried away by thoughts of the future, past, worries,or tasks you must complete. This is okay and a normal part of mindfulness, as your mind will naturally wander. When this happens, you simply bring your mind back to the present moment to remain focused. The exercise of mindfulness is simply bringing your focus back time and again to the present.

5.   When your mind wanders be kind to yourself. Don't judge your thoughtsor the fact that your mind has wandered. Simply recognize that your thoughts have wandered, and then come back to the present.

6.   You can exercise this either normally, as stated here, or you can includesome deep breathing exercises, as well. You will find that with the addition of deep breathing you can achieve an

even greater state of calmness and more easily pull yourself back to the present after your mind has wandered.

Now that you understand the most basic mindfulness exercise let's explore other forms of mindfulness therapy that you might utilize. Some of these vary in difficulty, but if you slowly work into it, you will find it becomes easier.

Deep Breathing

There are many benefits of including deep breathing into your mindfulness exercises. This exercise has been shown to help lower blood pressure, reduce stress, and decrease heart rate. While stressful situations often trigger the body's fight or flight response, deep breathing is able to calm the sympathetic nervous system, lower adrenaline, and return the body back to its normal state. This is helpful, because while the fight or flight response is needed in times of danger when we are safe but stressed it causes strain on the body. This is because the fight or flight response cannot tell the difference between true danger and stressful stations.

Therefore, if you are someone who struggles with stress or the fight or flight response regularly, then you will find that this method can greatly help return you to baseline. With deep breathing you can activate the body's natural relaxation response, promoting healing and a profoundly calm state.

Two forms of deep breathing include belly breathing and the four-seven-eight method. First, begin with belly breathing, and after you are adjusted to this you can move on to the following method, which is a little more difficult.

Four-Seven-Eight Breathing:

1. Sit or lay down somewhere comfortable. Using the belly breathing method, set one hand on the belly and the other on your chest.

2. Taking a deep breath from your belly through your nose silently count tothe number four.

3. After breathing in, count to the number seven while holding your breath.

4. After holding your breath breathe out completely while counting to thenumber eight. By the time you finish counting you should try to have all of the air out of your lungs.

5. Repeat this process three to seven times, until you feel a deep state ofcalmness.

6. Notice how you are feeling after completing the exercise and take note of any improvements.

Body Scan

The body scan method of mindfulness is a wonderful way to relax and calm your mind. However, it is about more than just being calm. Rather, this exercise requires a person to become aware of the different regions of their body. During this process, you become attuned to how each portion of your body feels, without trying to change it. You are simply present and aware. This allows you to get in touch with your body, release the daily stress of needing to accomplish tasks, and let go of pent-up emotions.

This form of mindfulness, like others, also promotes a state of focus. By switching your focus between the different regions of your body you are training your mind to be able to focus on different factors on command more easily.

You begin the body scan exercise by lying flat on your back with your arms next to you and palms facing upward. Your legs should be relaxed with your feet slightly apart. While this method is ideally done while laying down, feel free also to try doing it while sitting in a comfortable chair. If you choose to do this exercise sitting, then ensure your feet are sleeping solidly on the floor and your palms are facing upward.

Whether sitting or standing, be sure to stay as still as possible during the entire duration of the exercise. If you must move at one point, then move delivery while remaining aware of how it feels, your position, and remain in a deeply calm state.

After you are comfortable to become aware of your breathing, notice its rhythm and how it feels while it comes in and out of your lungs. As it enters and exits your nostril, experience how it feels to take air in and then fully expel it. While you want to become aware of your breathing, don't try to change it. During this time you aren't practicing deep breathing exercises or trying to alter how you usually breathe. Simply breathe in your normal way while remaining completely focused and aware of it.

Once you are fully aware of your breathing, move onto how your body feels. You want to notice your temperature against that of the environment, the texture of the cloth against your skin, the pressure of what you are sitting or lying on against your body. If any areas of your body are sore, tingling, or feel either light or heavy bring them to your attention. Note any areas of your body that are feeling hypersensitive of lack sensation.

After you have created a general state of awareness of your body begin to note every area of your body down from your toes up to your head. You always want to start from the lower portions of the body and then move upward.

A typical body scan includes focusing on these body parts in order:

Toes

Feet and ankles

Calves

Knees

Thighs

Pelvic area

Abdomen

Chest

Lower back

Upper back

Fingers

Hands and wrists

Arms

Neck

Face and head

Once you have completed your body scan for five to seven minutes, note how you feel, both physically and mentally. By understanding how this exercise helps you, then you will better know when to utilize it in the future.

Create a Safe Place

When beginning this exercise, you first want to create a sense of calmness and peace deep within. You can do this by sitting in a quiet and comfortable location. Close your eyes and simply focus on your breathing for one or two minutes. You don't have to exercise deep breathing; you simply want to be aware of your breathing and focus on nothing else. Once you have focused on your breathing for a minute or two expand your focus so that you are feeling the sensations of your entire body. You want to exercise this for about a minute until you find yourself in a state of deep calmness.

Feel that deep calmness? Once you find that peace and safety remain with your eyes closed, but imagine looking around yourself. What do you see when you look around with your mind's eye? Imagine a calm and peaceful place, anywhere that you feel most comfortable. This location may be a meadow with a brook, a forest with tall trees and damp leaves, an abandoned castle in the middle of a forest filled with old books and plants, a calm beach at sunset, or even your grandparent's house where you would visit on holiday.

Wherever your calm place is, focus on what you can see and feel there. Do you feel the sun on your skin? The breeze gently blowing your hair? Water from the side brushing back and forth on your feet? The warmth of fire against your face? The spines of worn ancient books against your fingertips? The warmth of the oven warming your entire body? Focus on the environment and notice everything you can feel in this safe place.

After you create a strong connection of what you can feel, focus on what you can hear. Do you hear birds calling? Ocean waves crashing against the shore? Fire crackling as it burns the wood? A hand beater mixing cake batter? Book pages turning? Animals in the distance calling to each other? Soft music?

Next, focus on the sense of smell. Do you smell the salty waves of the ocean? Fresh pine and jasmine? Dusty books? Smoke from the bonfire? Vanilla or chocolate cake as it cooks in the oven? The musty scent of a large cat?

Allow your entire body to relax as you imagine yourself in this safe space. Let the muscles in your neck, shoulders, and face go limp. Relax your arms and legs. Feel free to smile as you enjoy being surrounded in your safe space.

Lastly, imagine that not only do you enjoy your safe place but that this place enjoys having you in its presence, as well. When you arrive in this location both you and your safe space experience joy. You and this place share a deep emotional connection. Whenever you are stressed or need to feel at peace, love, or safe, you can come to this place to experience rejuvenation.

The Compassionate State

You will find that completing this exercise can help you develop a better sense of self. This exercise will also help you to develop more compassion over time, which you can then use on yourself and those around you.

To begin this exercise, once again create a peaceful and calm state. To do this sit or lay somewhere comfortable and focus on your natural breathing. Don't worry about deep breathing exercise or altering your breathing. You simply want to focus on how you naturally breathe.

After your body and mind have calmed and become focused, you can begin the exercise. Begin by imagining yourself as a compassionate person, who can feel, think, and act in a compassionate manner. Think of the qualities of compassion, such as warmth, wisdom, strength, and responsibility. Fantasize that you possess these qualities.

First, imagine that you have these qualities starting with wisdom. This deep sense of wisdom originates from a fundamental understanding of the mind, body, and nature of life.

Next, after you fully feel the quality of wisdom begin to imagine that you have a compassionate strength. Imagine that you have the strength to understand not only your own struggles but the struggles of others, as well. In a non-judgmental way, you can be tolerant, sensitive, and withstand struggles. Allow your body to naturally change postures in a way that reflects this compassionate strength.

After you understand wisdom and strength focus on feeling the element of warmth. Imagine that you show warmth and kindness to both yourself and others. Feel that you can reach out to others with warmth, imagining what it must feel like. Envision yourself talking to someone with warmth and kindness, noticing the tone of voice you use while completing this exercise using an expression that portrays this warmth.

Lastly, visualize that you have a strong sense of responsibility. You have no interest in blaming, judging, or condemning others or yourself; you simply wish to help everyone through their difficult circumstances. Remember to hold onto your warmth, strength, and wisdom. Fully commit yourself to be wholly compassionate. You may not possess all of these qualities at this time. You may not be a very compassionate person. That's okay. If you visualize yourself having these qualities and work towards gaining them, then you will slowly grow into them. Nobody will become passionate overnight, you simply have to keep working toward your goal and you will get there. Being wise, strong, responsible, and warm takes exercise, as does everything else.

Flowing Compassion

Sit or lay somewhere quiet and calm, where you know you won't be disturbed. Focus on calm natural breathing until you are relaxed. Then, think back to a time when you are compassionate, kind, and caring to either another human or an animal. Although, try to think of a situation in which the animal or human was happy. You do not want a situation in which they were distressed, as you might begin to focus on the stress of the situation rather than the compassion.

While visualizing the situation, focus on the feelings of kindness and warmth, on your desire to help the other human or animal. Your focus shouldn't be how the animal or human responses to your compassion, but rather your intentions of kindness. Visualize yourself slowly growing as you imagine the compassion you were expressing. Imagine growing wiser, stronger, warmer, calmer, and more responsible, able to help the other person or animal better.

Focus on your body; remember the experience of how it feels to be kind and compassionate. Allow the warmth to flow through your body while you notice the real compassion and well-wishes for the person or animal to fully flourish. Consider the kind and compassionate words you might say your tone of voice, and actions you took to help. Visualize how nice it felt to be compassionate. Lastly, focus completely on your desire to be compassionate, helpful, and kind. Notice the feeling of expansion, the flow of warmth, with wise words and actions, the kind tone of voice. After you finish focusing on this, you may consider taking notes on how it felt. By using this exercise, you will find that you increase your desire to be compassionate, as well as your knowledge in how to act on this desire. As you continue to exercise this exercise, your compassion will slowly increase, and you will become better at directing your compassion both inward and outward.

Focusing Compassion Inward

You have both an anxious self and a troubled self. You can use this inner compassion mindfulness technique to help direct compassion inward. But, while you can direct the compassion to both of these selves, you can only do one at a time. Therefore, if you wish to direct compassion toward both selves, you will have to follow through with the exercise twice, focusing on one of the selves in turn.

In order to use this technique, it will help if you have first learned how to use the Compassionate State technique, in which you visualize yourself as being full of compassion.

The Troubled Self:

Firstly, you will want to sit or lay down in a quiet and peaceful area. Close your eyes and notice the feeling of your body. Focus on reaching the compassionate state, ensuring your facial expression is one conveying warmth.

Imagine you are outside of yourself, watching your actions as though you were watching someone else or a recording. Imagine watching yourself waking up and getting out of bed in the morning, moving around the house, and preparing for a usual day. As you watch this "recording" of yourself remember to feel compassion and kindness toward you that you are watching.

Notice the self-critical and troubling thoughts and emotions you in the recording are expressing. Pay attention to their struggle with compassion without letting it weight or bog you down. Continue watching with your compassionate self with the intention of sharing warmth, kindness, strength, wisdom, and aid.

If your compassionate self begins to fade away then release the "recording" of yourself and go back to the compassionate state exercise. Regain your sense of peace and compassion. Find your gentle expression full of warmth. Then, after you regain this, you may go back to the recording and watching yourself

By completing this exercise regularly, you can find a more objective and compassionate view of yourself. You will be able to see your struggles, the difficult things you go through, and appreciate yourself for them. Through completing this exercise, you can become more intuitive and accepting of yourself.

The Anxious Self:

Whether you have been diagnosed with an anxiety disorder or simply struggle with anxiety at points in your life, this version of the technique will help you manage and release some anxiety. This is because by finding compassion for your anxious self, you will understand how to manage your anxiety better and are less likely to punish yourself for experiencing it.

Spend a few minutes to tap into your compassionate self. Feel the warm expression on your face, the sense of kindness, wisdom, strength, and responsibility. Focus on this sense of compassion and peace while you breathe normally.

Following, envision yourself in a situation where you are anxious. This may be a past situation or an imagined situation that has not previously occurred. While imagining this stressful situation, remember to maintain your compassionate self.

Move outside of your body and watch yourself as though you were watching a recording. Notice how you become anxious, how you feel and act. Find understanding, compassion, and empathy for this anxious self.

Fantasize about how you would like to help your anxious self and what you might say to them to lessen the anxiety. You may choose to encourage them, recognize their ability to get through the struggle or validate their emotions. Whatever you choose to say, let it come from a place of compassion, kindness, and helpfulness.

As time gradually moves in this vision, see the anxiety slowly reducing and lessening until it is completely gone. Experience how it feels to come through the situation and offer your anxious self some understanding, encouragement, and kindness. Express to them the courage they showed by getting through the period of anxiety.

Later on, whenever you are in a situation that causes an increase in anxiety, exercise using deep or rhythmic breathing. Slow down and remind yourself of the compassionate self. See yourself through these eyes and acknowledge the struggle you are going through. Encourage and be kind to yourself.

As you can see, there are many types of medication and mindfulness. In this book, we have only been able to touch on a small number of the techniques, but if you use them regularly, you will soon experience many great benefits.

The important habits that can change your life

Given enough time, we can probably think of many helpful habits that we'd like to be able to exercise every day. But realistically speaking, we can only focus on a handful of habits at any given time. It does take real effort and commitment to cultivate a habit, and so, if we wish to get good results, we must be selective in choosing which habits to work on.

Below is a list of some good habits worth cultivating. This list takes into account what psychologists and lifestyle gurus believe to be essential attitudes and actions that help to create a happy and meaningful life. The habits included aren't listed in any particular order. Feel free to choose any one of them, or a few, that you think can make a difference in your life.

Habit #1: Positive thinking

The habit of thinking positively is an important one that can support the formation of other useful habits. It is therefore a very desirable habit and general attitude of mind to have. When you think positively and with optimism, you are naturally motivated to try out new things and work towards any goal. This frame of mind gives you added energy. It doesn't hurt that it also makes you an easier person to get along with. Naturally, everyone enjoys the company of a happy and optimistic person more than that of a dour or cynical individual.

Thinking positively also comes in handy when you're trying to get rid of bad habits. A bad habit, such as smoking or mindless overeating, can be very difficult to eliminate because it is so ingrained in the person. He can easily become discouraged and give up before even giving it a real try. But when he thinks positively, there's a greater chance he will keep trying until he eventually conquers the habit.

To get into the habit of positive thinking, always look towards the bright side. Anticipate good results, and prepare to work hard for them. Also very importantly, watch out for negative thoughts. These can come from other people, but more often, they come from within your own self. Negative selftalk is very common, and psychologists say that it is a huge source of unhappiness for a lot of people. So try to catch yourself when negative thoughts strike. Here are some examples to be wary of:

It's too difficult.

I can't possibly do it.

I'm too _____ (fat, thin, shy, young, old, short, tall, etc.) to be able to do it.

What will people say?

I'll just embarrass myself if I go through with it.

It's a waste of time.

It's not worth it.

I'm not worth it.

I'm not ready.

Whenever you think of these or other negative thoughts that resemble them, take a deep breath, and pause for a while. Ask yourself if those thoughts arise out of fear, laziness, a low self-esteem, or a natural resistance to change. Then simply refuse to believe in the negative thought and proceed with what you were planning to do. Tell yourself that you can do it, and that it will be done.

Habit #2: Keeping a gratitude journal

A gratitude journal is simply a notebook where you record things that you are grateful for every day. You write on it something that made you happy that day. It can be a kind gesture that someone did for you, an event that took place, a state of things, a certain feeling, a possession or object you value, an experience—anything that you are grateful for. Even if nothing special actually happened on a given day, you can still think of many things to be grateful for, such as your health, the good weather, having friends and family that care for you, the birds singing outside, the smell of a freshly mowed lawn, and so on. The point of having a gratitude journal is to focus on the positive things in your life. When you do this habitually, you will develop an attitude of positivity, optimism, hope and gratitude. Having this mindset will make you a happier person, regardless of what's actually happening in your life. When bad or sad things happen, you can read some entries in your gratitude journal and be reminded that life still has so much to offer.

A notebook that you write on is the best way to keep a gratitude journal. But should you wish to, you can use apps on your mobile phone or computer that function as an electronic gratitude journal.

Habit #3: Eliminating the non-essential

This means living simply and cutting out extraneous activities and objects. To do this, first identify what is essential to you, what is most important, or what gives you the greatest happiness. Then eliminate everything else.

Another way of going about it is putting everything through a litmus test. For example, ask yourself if an activity is essential, important, or joy-giving. If it isn't, then don't do it. Extend the same test to other things in your life, such as relationships, possessions, emails and social media, and so on. Before making a purchase, apply the test. Before committing to a social engagement, apply the same test. Then act accordingly.

Make simplifying your life a habit. When you do so, you can really focus on the important things. And you will also have immensely more time and energy for them. You can then build the life that you really want. **Habit #4. Exercising**

Are you shaking your head right now and wondering how exercising is one of the top habits to cultivate? You shouldn't, because there are a lot of reasons why exercise is very important. Here are some of them:

> Exercise keeps you healthy.
>
> It prevents or cures depression and other mood disorders, as well as a host of diseases and medical conditions.

It makes you happy.

It fosters optimism and positive thinking.

It makes you feel good about yourself, boosting your self confidence.

It relieves stress.

It clears your mind.

It is relaxing.

It makes you sleep better.

It promotes creativity and mental health.

As such, do try to have some form of exercise as a habit. It can be something as simple as talking a walk or a jog every other day. Or you can join a gym or a sports club. It will do wonders for your health, and you'll be a much happier person too.

Habit #5. Single-tasking

This may sound unfamiliar to you, but it's just the opposite of multi-tasking. Single-tasking simply means working on only one thing (a single task) at a time. It is life-changing, and it results in a tremendous boost in productivity. Studies reveal that contrary to popular belief, multitasking isn't an efficient method of getting things done in the workplace. A person is more effective and efficient when he does only one piece of work at a time, rather than when he juggles several tasks together.

When a person single-tasks, he also experiences less stress. Offices and workplaces where people single-task are calmer, happier and more efficient spaces.

Another benefit of single-tasking is that it encourages focus and mindfulness. Because the person is doing only one thing, he can focus completely on it, increasing the likelihood that he'll do an excellent job. In addition to performing excellently, he also learns to cultivate the habit of mindfulness, or being attuned to the here and now. This, in itself, can be a simple form of meditation with many wonderful benefits to the person practicing it.

Habit #6: Spending money on experiences, not material things

Possessions come and go, break and fall, go out of trend, and so on. On the other hand, experiences turn into memories that you can cherish for the sleep of your life. If you want the secret to happiness, this is it: Spend money on experiences, not possessions. This claim is backed up by extensive psychological research. Research findings show that material possessions do not provide life-long happiness because of three things:

1. There are always new possessions to be had.

2. Our expectations are ever increasing.

3. We are always comparing our possessions to what somebody else has.

In other words, material possessions will always disappoint us.

Experiences, meanwhile, have the power to inspire us, even after they're done. They become a part of our identity, shaping us to become better versions of ourselves. They are also more special because they are fleeting, which gives us a sense of anticipation and excitement for what is yet to come. In addition, your experiences are unique to you and you alone. Even if you travel with a friend, your experience of that trip is still different from his. Therefore, comparisons do not really matter. While new and better versions of gadgets, cars and other material possessions are created, your experiences will remain unique and special to you.

Habit #7. Being kind

Yes, you're reading it right. Kindness is a habit, and one that every person should cultivate.

Being kind means doing a kind act for someone, anyone. It can be for a friend, a family member, co-worker, or a total stranger. It doesn't have to involve giving away money or something with a monetary value. It just means being compassionate and friendly. It can mean volunteering in a charitable event, lending a helping hand, patting someone in the back for a job well done, or listening to a person who needs to vent.

Opportunities for kind acts are not hard to find. They could be right inside your home or your workplace. Grab the chance to be kind whenever you can, and you won't just be benefitting the other person. You'll also feel good, and you'll feel connected to another human being. That's always a lovely thing.

Work on being kind as you would on any other habit that you'd like to cultivate. Every day, take every chance you get to be kind to someone else. After a while, you'll witness profound changes happening in your life. For one thing, you'll feel a deeper kind of peace and calmness. People will react to you differently and—not surprisingly—treat you more kindly. What you give out will really come back to you. That's karma.

Habit #8: Making lists

This is a practical habit that will increase your productivity and keep you organized. Lists are useful not only as visual reminders, but also to help you to plan ahead and clarify your priorities. When you list something down, that means you have given it some thought, and that you consider it to be important. You can make lists of many things, such as tasks that you need to do, grocery items or supplies that you need to buy, people you need to contact or buy gifts for (on holidays such as Christmas), and interesting ideas that come to you at unexpected moments. It is therefore a good exercise (another habit to learn!) to always bring with you a small notebook where you can write down these lists and reminders, at any time that an idea or item to include occurs to you. If you wish, you can use your smart phone to jot down your lists. There are many apps for list-making that you can download and use. Another benefit of making lists is that it gives you the satisfaction of crossing out items that have been completed. There is a simple pleasure in this that encourages greater productivity and that just makes you feel good about yourself.

Habit #9: Waking up early

Each person's schedule is different, so it's difficult to pin down a specific time that everyone would consider as "early." It is ideal if you can wake up before or at sunrise and enjoy the quietude of that time. Everyone else is still asleep, and the world is quiet and at peace. It is a wonderful, beautiful time to do something meaningful, or to just enjoy quietly. However, if you cannot get up this early, then just consider waking up at least 30 minutes earlier than your usual waking-up time.

Think of this habit as allowing yourself an extra 30 minutes or so of the day for special me-time. You can do with this time whatever you wish, but we suggest that it be something meaningful or special. If you are a prayerful person, use this time to pray, meditate or exercise gratefulness. If you are a sporty person, this time is perfect for an outdoor run or yoga/tai-chi session (you'll enjoy seeing the sunrise as a bonus). If you prefer to use this time to get some important work done, then go ahead and use it to plan your day or to make a list of the tasks that you want to accomplish.

Doing something useful, beautiful, or meaningful first, right after you wake up, will set the tone for the remainder of the day. It is a great start to what probably would be a great day.

Conclusion

Remind yourself to work on the things that you are able to do, not those that you cannot right now. This will give you more self-confidence and will help you to be aware of your value and the immediate power you have.

One of the secrets to long-term happiness is to make sure you have yourself around other people who are happy it's contagious! In an effort to obtain long-term happiness we have to reprogram your brain from the negative mindset to a positive mindset.

Relationships with God, our spouses and our children come from having virtue and how you treat people in your life and showing respect towards others is showing integrity. Displaying awareness will ensure that your words will be an encouragement to those who hear them. When you love someone it is better not to criticize them because criticism can kill the joy of a relationship and take the focus off of the positive aspects. Adopting spiritual beliefs improves lives, well-being, and physical health and also helps us to cope with small daily life stresses as well as major traumas. One of the easiest ways to improve your life is to get enough sleep and drink plenty of water. People who do not get enough sleep are usually they're stuck on their negative thoughts affects their ability to focus on positive things.

They also tend to engagement in more negative thinking, they worry obsessively and they actually attach some of their stress onto other people. Not getting enough sleep is bad for your immune system and your physical health when you sleep better it helps recover from injuries quicker and speeds up the recovery process after surgery.